ADDICTED TO GRIEF

ADDICTED TO GRIEF

Life After Alexus Died

Amelia Ochoa

Universal-Publishers
Irvine • Boca Raton

Addicted to Grief: Life After Alexus Died

Universal Publishers, Inc.
Irvine • Boca Raton
USA • 2024
www.Universal-Publishers.com

ISBN: 978-1-62734-470-8 (pbk.)
ISBN: 978-1-62734-471-5 (ebk.)
ISBN: 978-1-62734-472-2 (aud.)

Typeset by Medlar Publishing Solutions Pvt Ltd, India
Cover design by Ivan Popov

Library of Congress Cataloging-in-Publication Data

Names: Ochoa, Amelia, 1978- author.
Title: Addicted to grief : life after Alexus died / Amelia Ochoa.
Description: Irvine : Universal-Publishers, [2024]
Identifiers: LCCN 2024008381 (print) | LCCN 2024008382 (ebook) | ISBN 9781627344708 (paperback) | ISBN 9781627344715 (ebook)
Subjects: LCSH: Grief. | Parental grief. | Children--Death.
Classification: LCC BF575.G7 O2583 2024 (print) | LCC BF575.G7 (ebook) | DDC 155.9/37085--dc23/eng/20240305
LC record available at https://lccn.loc.gov/2024008381
LC ebook record available at https://lccn.loc.gov/2024008382

Grief has no discrimination.

It does not value socioeconomic classes
in any way, shape, or form.
Whatever your creed or origin, grief will find you.
It sees no color or gender. It will not skip over
any religions or ethnicities. Grief will find you.
It is inevitable. In order or even in an untimely matter,
grief is real.

Don't stop fighting grief and reclaim your right now.

Get help and seek counsel from a higher being.
I call Him God. Whatever you call Him, seek and
you shall find counsel and resolutions. Some resolutions
come from churches of different denominations, others
from hidden messages. Listen for one.

—Amelia Ochoa

Knock, and it shall be opened unto you ...

—Matthew 7:7

TABLE OF CONTENTS

ACKNOWLEDGMENTS

I would like to acknowledge God for giving me the strength and courage to write this book and to help me overcome this addiction. First and foremost, all honor and glory to Him because without Him, I am lost. I would like to give God more credit for placing particular angels in front of me when I thought I could no longer stand up. You know who you are. Essie and Vernice Dockins, Tia Panchita, Grandma Leonar, and Tia Nena—resting in peace—Jada C. Harris, Shawn L. Lawrence Jr., Cha'Rayia K. Johnson. Momma and Papi. Ervin King, Maliyah G. Childs. Dane C. Scott and Cameron Smiley. Many other angels. Those who inspire me still (singers and songwriters): Kirk Franklin, Maverick City Music, Jackalyn Carr, Tye Tribbett, Rod Wave, Aaliyah, Anthony Brown, and Group TherAPy. Your music got me through so much! To Angela Navarro and Sarah Jake Roberts, who ignited the birth of this book. Pastor and First Lady of United Baptist Church of OKC, First Southern Baptist Church of OKC family. The Bible. To Jimmy Mendoza, MBA, and to Ms. Dane Norwood and Riki Mendoza for editing. To Meagan Hughes, Antonio Ochoa Jr., Veronica Norwood, Katrina Jones, Veronica Harris-Rodriguez, and Blanca for your input and words. Kendra Skanes Wright. The Bible, Elisabeth

Kübler-Ross, Galen, Aristotle, The Society for Humanistic Psychology, Division 32 of the American Psychological Association, Evermore.org, the University of Texas, Niran Al-Agba, and MND Family.

To my siblings, Veronica (Danny), Gracie (Jesse), Jimmy (Shawnda), Rachel (Nardo), Saraih, and Blanca. To Takisha, Yalonda, Marcus (Timisha), Earnest, Glenn, Michael, Chauncey, and Justin (Allison), who have helped me maintain my life through comments and prayers. To LaDwana, Anita McClain, and family for helping plan my daughter's service when we could not; I am forever grateful. My nieces and nephews, her cousins. To the Ochoas, Garcias, and Wrights. To my mother, Juanita, rest in heaven, who prayed for us before we were even born; to my mother-in-law Diane King and to Momma Patty (Matt). To my children, Alexus, Aniah, Ayissa, Amanee, and Marlon II; and to my husband, Marlon King-Dockins, for keeping us in church, no matter what. To the Kings and Dockins who helped with the upbringing of Alexus. May God continue to bless you all. To Cortez Wright for showing Alexus a new life. To my amazing Grandmother Prici. To Tron (Sherfonda), to James W. and Terrence N.; I know your mothers are resting easy. To Trey Alexander for the inspiration. MD and Quavy, tell your story.

PREFACE

The journey of writing this book and traversing the concepts of grief was self-therapeutic. My mind opened to things I had never even considered. If I, a grown woman, with God's inspiring grasp on me, overcame the most inconceivable trauma and an unbiased addiction to grief, perhaps my story can help you through yours.

I had to reevaluate my life with the life tools instilled in me to help myself and my children process their grief and introduce them to tools of their own. Now, eight years later, I find myself making up for lost time. In doing so, I reflected on the everyday challenges and struggles our community, this community of grieving parents, faced.

We all are accustomed to daily challenges and struggles that may not define us today but that shape who we are. Our past follows us; it makes our stories relatable.

To all parents dealing with the grief of losing a child, may God continue to provide peace and comfort to you, mind, body, and soul.

MY STORY

In 2015, during the early morning hours of September 28, I got a phone call that changed my life forever. Hours prior to this tragic call, I had left my nineteen-year-old daughter, Alexus, at the hospital. She appeared to be doing well and, I thought, in good hands. Alexus was a vibrant, healthy young woman. She was an athlete and a scholar in her second year of college. But she was much more than that. She was my firstborn child. She was a big sister, a cousin, a niece, a best friend, a girlfriend, and a granddaughter who was loved and accepted by all those who knew her. She was a walking inspiration with a friendly personality, and she changed the lives of many, young and old. She saw the good in everything and everyone. She made people around her feel welcomed and important, and she valued life and lived every day as if it were her last. She overcame many obstacles and carried a presence within her that was so big it shined through her soul and reached those who needed it the most. She graced this earth and will never be forgotten.

Although Alexus's spirit has ascended into heaven, I am reminded almost daily of how encouraging she still is. She inspires so many that, even as I type this story, I can hear her soft-spoken voice and enormous heart telling me to share this story so I can help others like me and like you, because this is a journey we—you and I—are all too familiar with.

I never wanted to be a part of this community, but here I am. Here we are.

The commonality between us is the lives that were taken from us too soon but will never be forgotten. Both sadly and realistically, what we share may seem unfathomable to most. Some do not even think about or comprehend our existence. Some cannot get past the point of imagining going through this, not fully, the way we are going through it. As we continue our journeys, many will think of us, but those who are not a part of this group cannot truly understand what burying a child is like. Many may know us but have no idea what we go through on a day-to-day basis (at times, I do not even want to walk in my own shoes—but here I am). There are many whose lives go on while we are left to pick up the pieces of an undesired new normal that we must learn how to accept—if we can at all. I was someone who looked at acceptance last.

Throughout this book, you will find space to help you rid your mind and heart of things that have held you back within your grieving process or that consume you. Holding things in is unhealthy. Please allow these spaces to help you identify what you may be struggling with. This is your personal space, so use the strength within you to take the first steps of alleviating your grief or any other grief-addicted substances that are still inside you. Write down more feelings that you hold. What were your thoughts after you received the information that brought you into this community? (Come back and revisit your answers, as I did).

What were you doing in your life when it was paused, when you received the news of your child's passing? Use this moment to tell your story.

I was a wife and a mother to five beautiful children. I was involved in many community activities. I was living a life that most would say was normal. I loved my life and everything about it. My life had normal strain, just like anyone else's. I never thought I would get a call while I was asleep, after having just left the hospital and spoken to my daughter, who seemed fine. Prior to that moment, we were out of town as a family playing basketball—just another normal weekend—and Alexus stayed home to study for a test. This was the first time she did not come with us.

As I was processing her death, I had so much inside me that I pushed it away. It would manifest itself again, and I would push it back down farther instead of addressing my thoughts and feelings, which I now identify as parts of my grief addiction. I found that writing helped. Sometimes we are not ready to talk to someone, but there is something about being able to write freely that helps the most. We can come back and see growth. While reading and answering, I will speak about my personal answers so we can get through this together.

When I heard the news about Alexus, I could not believe what I was hearing. I frantically prepared myself to curse out the hospital when I got there for giving me the wrong news. But once I found out they were telling the truth, I had no idea what I was about to face.

I was so mad at God. I could not believe that out of all the times He answered prayers, He could not come through for me on this. I did not want to know Him nor talk to Him.

I did not like half of the comments that people were making about why they thought my daughter had passed away. I heard the most insensitive and outlandish things being said about my daughter's passing.

I did not realize how the negativity was about to affect my life, and at that time, I didn't care. The negativity enraged me, but I was going through so much that I stopped listening outwardly. Yet still my ears took it in subliminally, and it filled my mind.

We all had a life prior to becoming a part of this community. That is what I would like us to remember. No one is ever ready for this type of change, but we can get back to where we need to be for ourselves and for our family members. We will get through this together. YOU ARE NOT ALONE! Please know that as I sit here, I hope that sharing the way I defeated my addiction to grief makes you understand how much we are in this together.

STAND WITH ME

I have taken a stand against grieving for my child.

I truly believe that if you can say those words along with me, you too have begun your journey in standing up against grief.

We all must learn to cope with the losses of such precious young lives. I am praying for you to understand that missing your child will ultimately be the hardest part of this process. Right now, as you take a stand on freeing yourself from the addiction to grief, become one of the strongest members of this community (Parents against Grieving Every Day).

This community continues to grow for many different reasons, but at its heart, the loss of a child brings us together. Whether the loss of a child was expected or not, our community knows that, no matter what, the child's death was untimely and true. I believe that before we became a part of this community, we had all probably considered the possibility of our children passing away when we would hear the news of someone else having to endure this unbearable pain. Though, even at that, our ability to fathom this pain was not as clear as the day we learned the most surreal news that would change us all forever.

NEWFOUND GRIEF

In my case, I got the phone call, and I have to be honest—once they got through to me, I was lost. I could not grasp the concept of the call. In my mind, the conversation that was taking place could not be true. I had to hang up and call the hospital back because I had just visited with my daughter hours before.

As I heard the hospital staff relaying the information to me, I could not make myself understand the language being spoken. I thought the hospital representative had the wrong person.

Once Alexus's identity was confirmed, I hung up the phone in disbelief. I began to pace back and forth, going over the information, trying to talk myself into believing the conversation. However, my mind denied the news.

My subconscious took over. I turned the shower on. Cold. I got in. I had to get back to myself, to wake up from this nightmare. But when the water cleared and reality returned, I still battled with what the hospital representatives and I had just discussed.

I woke up my husband, Alexus's father, but I was still in total shock. I do not even remember exactly what I told him. I guess things are sometimes better left forgotten, as you and I may both know. We needed to leave quickly, without waking up Alexus's four younger siblings. Once my husband was finally able to understand what I was telling him, we rushed to the hospital in hopes of finding our daughter in a much better position than we had been told.

We did not.

Alexus died in the early morning on Monday, September 28, 2015, and in that moment, my addiction to grief slowly began to overcome my mind and heart. It took over my mind, body, and soul. When she left the world, I assumed 20 percent of my heart left with her. (It may have left with her, but as I write this book, I reclaim that percentage because I need all my heart to get to where I am needed the most.) The math still does not make sense to me. I think nothing makes sense when you have just received the most devastating and tragic news possible. At that time, I had no idea and did not understand what this newfound grief was about to place on me. I found out that everything I had been told at the hospital was true, so why not begin to believe everything else that was about to unfold in my mind? My mind was challenging my thoughts already. This then started the mental distress, and I allowed all the negativity that came with it to house itself in my mind. Grief began to accomplish its purpose with all the other substances that came with it. I believe the enemy was mentally attacking my mind, causing my body and soul to shut down its strength as I was about to consume every substance (emotion) that grief gives a parent. My heart was too cold to handle any positivity. That was the most vulnerable time of my life. My mind and body felt an immense cold, sadness, and pain. An unbearable shudder swept through my soul, and grief entered my heart.

Grief had broken my soul to such a degree that I almost forgot about the family I still had. For a moment, I thought only about myself. I went into shock and then, immediately, and I switched to autopilot. I then thought of my other four children—but only briefly—because I could not handle what was transpiring within me. How could I handle the grief for someone else? My autopilot kicked in, and I resumed my life as though nothing had happened. I was in complete shock and denial. That shock and denial would contradict every grief-fueled emotion I was feeling.

Nevertheless, when my daughter passed away, I could not get past the thought—or even acknowledge—that anyone else had ever been through this or would ever go through the same things I was. Now, when I look back at those times, I know there were plenty of people experiencing the untimely death of a child. But at the time, I felt like the answers or help that I needed were beyond my understanding. The answers were out of my grasp because, as you and I know, in those moments, it is hard to retain information, especially if it is something we are not looking for. I needed answers as quickly as possible. I needed my daughter back, immediately. Perhaps I should have reached out for help. Honestly, I did not want to speak with anyone unless they were bringing back Alexus (which was impossible). I was so caught up in these new substances of grief that even when I did speak to someone, I could not retain the information. But what I did retain was the unknown addictions of the feelings and emotions that were consuming me.

Before I prepared a contemplation about how my advancement with the process of grief subsided within me, and after I let go of what happened to Alexus (without letting go of her), I did some research. I would like to state right now that I am not a certified or degree-holding psychologist. I am just a mother defeating grief, because I am determined that grief will not dictate who I am. I am a mother attempting to withstand or redirect my grief into a process that allows me to understand my newfound concepts on dealing with grief—especially for the death of my firstborn daughter, which was a tragedy I was not prepared for. You can get a glimpse of her passing in a book called *Patients at Risk: The Rise of the Nurse Practitioner and Physician Assistant in Healthcare*, by Dr. Niran Al-Agba and Dr. Rebekah Bernard.

As I was finding facts or theories about the stages of grieving, I came across a few free articles and videos. The psychologist Elisabeth Kübler-Ross studied adults who were terminally ill. She recognized five stages of grieving: denial, anger, bargaining, depression, and acceptance (DABDA). Those five stages of grieving evidently were theorized long ago and were challenged by some researchers a few years ago. Based on my own experiences, I agree with the challenge. Compared with the stages of grieving that I will illustrate within this book, the five stages of grieving may seem similar and sound familiar to you. Even more so, they may help you connect the way that some grieving processes flow. I would also like to state that these findings about grief were typical for adults who were given a certain amount of time left to live. In my research, I learned more about what appeared to be a chronological order of stages of grieving as I tried to identify my process with the stages of DABDA. It seemed to me to be a chronological order but was not clear in my research. To me, our grieving process is very different; I know we identify with DABDA, but it is not about chronological order to us. Grief is the most life-changing uphill battle that many of us face on a day-to-day basis. Although at times grieving can be considered a roller coaster, I would actually describe my grief process as a tornado.

Honestly, I would have been better off with the roller coaster. At least then I would have been better prepared, or I could have gotten off the ride when it was over. Don't you agree? A roller coaster gives you the option to get back on when you are ready. My grieving and mourning for Alexus were like a tornado in that I never knew when it was going to hit. The news warns us when tornadoes are coming, but even when we take cover, there may be some debris to clean up. Sit back for a moment, pause, and ask yourself, what was my grieving like? Or better yet How is it now?

Please use the next pages to write down your feelings over time. Throughout this book, I describe my feelings, and within the paragraphs you have just read, I speak briefly of my own. As you write yours, please continue to read and see what other feelings and ideas that may make you stay in the grieving process.

Survivor's remorse is typically defined by some type of traumatic event that leads to post-traumatic stress disorder (PTSD). When we lose a loved one and we are left as survivors, we often feel some type of remorse or guilt for still being alive. While I can agree with that definition, I can also say that because my daughter lived a short life, I found that the term "survivor's remorse" might fit the way I was feeling.

For many years, I struggled with grief addiction because of my daughter's death. It still feels wrong and unnatural to say that my daughter is dead. I experienced guilt that followed me everywhere and came back every time I thought I could be happy. This remorse and guilt would take my happiness away because my daughter was not there to share the experience of joy with me and our family. Or at least not physically, because once you accept death, you know in essence that your loved one is always near.

As the guilt grew, it began to give me undesired doses of mental anguish. I would spend time thinking about how I had not been there to help my daughter or even hold her hand when she may have been scared. I hate to think of it, but it is my reality. When a child (even an adult child) is frightened or frantic and does not understand what is happening or the situation at hand, a parent is needed for comfort. Those instances are what a child and a parent are supposed to face together. They gain comfort from each another, and the child is left with assurance that everything will be okay. Even more so, they are perhaps spiritually comforted by prayer or shared knowledge from the parent. But I was not with my daughter during those moments.

As I progressed with the guilt, I thought of how my daughter's future had been extinguished, and I asked why she had to leave instead of me. I knew she would have been a great mother one day. As this guilt continued to take over my mind and my heart, I began to deal with why I survived and she did not, despite knowing that her death and my presence were not connected. I was not with my daughter when she passed. But her life's ending left me beyond traumatized. I felt devastated that her life had ended so abruptly and was so short. She was only nineteen, and I was thirty-seven. Even at my young age, I was remorseful because I still thought that I had lived long enough, at least longer than she had. I often thought about us trading places, even though it was impossible.

I share this state of mind because once I got to the point where I could process grief differently, I began to think back on some of my feelings and could not disregard the feelings I held. I needed to remember them and revisit them in this book in order to see my own growth from the time I received the news of Alexus's death to now. I hope that this explanation can help those of you who may feel the same way. As I stated before, I knew parents who had buried their children, and yet I still felt like these feelings were mine alone.

I suggest reaching out to someone you know who has perhaps been through the same thing. Keep a line of communication open as much as possible whenever you are able or ready to retain information, even if it is subliminally.

It can be hard.

FEELING DIFFERENT

Feeling different was hard for me and still is. Please do not let anyone tell you how to grieve. Grieving is truly a personal process, but I can only suggest that you take it one day at a time and look to the future. Admittedly, this was something I could not do for eight years. I cannot believe I am here now, feeling so differently about her death. It surprises me how the love of my family and my God, your God, has gotten me this far. With every part of my being, I am so grateful that God helped me process these experiences. He allowed me to see the inspiration in front of me and leave the torment behind. I can also see how inspiring I can be to myself. And I can see how my daughter is in heaven, looking upon me, smiling. The strength that I found deep down inside me and Alexus's inspiration, along with that of my family, also still run within me. This is why I want to share this book with you. Think of how inspiring your child would still want you to be. They would want you to carry on with your life, spreading memories and laughter and being as inspiring as your inspirations. The last thing that a child wants to see is your sadness or disappointment at not being able to move on with your life.

God created a natural mechanism with our ever-so-simple and small, yet complex and huge minds. The brain is thought of as an organ made of soft tissue rather than as a muscle like our hearts. It functions as the coordinating center of feelings (emotional or physical), along with being our intellectual center and the location of activity from our nervous system. Within the different types of nervous systems, any pain or sensation can send messages and signals to the brain.

After much research, I feel fully confident about how the mind, body, and soul relate to grieving. I believe it is important to understand how the brain functions, how each process works, and how it affects our being.

After my struggle with my addiction to grief, I found answers.

Through other findings, I came to understand that our brain is the most important organ in the body. Studies also show that the brain houses how we approach every concept available, how emotions are incorporated with one another, and how our personality collides with our being and with the levels of our consciousness and subconscious. It makes perfect sense that when the hurt or pain sensations go through our body and heart, they are relayed to the brain, which then sends signals back and forth to each other through neurons. For example, when we feel pain and we take medication, the medication is meant to stop or block those feelings. But there was no medication for me that stopped this pain; it just coated what I was feeling then and actually caused me to notice other substances of the addiction I was about to face.

The philosophers Galen and Aristotle both believed that the heart not only serves as a center of the soul but also affects our feelings and reactions. The soul is the source of consciousness and life in the body. For some of us, our kids are now souls and spirits, but we still remain here in physical form. Whatever reason or purpose for this is, we have to make the most of it, maybe by consoling others who are in the same situation as us.

In defining what I researched of my firsthand encounters with grieving my child's passing, this is my conclusion: Grief is inevitable—some days are going to be sad, some good, and some better. Even after we accept our situation, missing our child will still be devastating and unequivocally the hardest part of grief; but once we are able to separate each emotion from the other, the battle will be easier.

My name is Amy Ochoa-Dockins, and I am a survivor of grief addiction.

Finding and exploring the five stages of grief gave me a better insight into my feelings because, as we are all aware, we are not alone. So, while trying to grasp these stages, can we be so vulnerable that our desperation leads us to place our own emotions and feelings into the cookie-cutter formula of these five stages, into an order of operations that we must follow? That happened to me, and ultimately I decided to face grief with my own mind, set my own process, and decide that no one can tell me how to grieve. There will be no order of operations for me.

Even as I sit here thinking of all I have been through; my mind is continuously asking me questions about how and why I feel the way I do. Even after my extensive research, a lot of questions remain, and adjusting to my old new normal takes practice, time, and effort. Sometimes my mind may even bring up traumatic experiences. At those times, I can choose to respond, or I can tell my mind to stop thinking of things that draw in unwanted feelings. We are only human, and it is natural for us to have and hold feelings, good or bad. We all struggle from time to time, which is natural. Do not ever think that what you are feeling about the death of your child is uncommon. Not the feelings or the act itself. According to statistics, that is what we are a part of now. You and me together. As I sit here and gather my thoughts, which my mind processes into information, I can still feel my mind wandering and turning while I'm sharing what I'd like to think is knowledge that can help you.

I sometimes battle to stay focused, and it can be challenging. Yet even when I do not think I have it in me, I know that God is the precursor and the ending of my life, and that is constant. He is consistently waiting for me when I fall behind. I also strongly believe that we all have tools within us that God has placed there. Ask yourself what your life was really about and how it was before that tragic day. I know my life was busy, happy, chaotic, flexible, and at times interrupted. Truthfully, right now, I would love to have any interruption other than the one I faced that fateful day. Before that day, all my family members were present, whether they were home or not. My life felt normal to me, and never in a million years did I think of how it would change. Now it is forever different but accepted, and I am able to move forward and continue to be the mother, sister, aunt, cousin, granddaughter, daughter, friend, and wife that I am meant to be. Life hits us, but so does death. Life continues after death, and so must we.

If I knew then what I know now, I would have appreciated even comprehending then or retaining real-time information. Unknowingly, this is what God was already sending me and equipping me with. I'd like to say, in reference to the previous sentence, as I was in the early stages of grieving and mourning, I was absent-minded yet present in conversation. God allowed me to retain this type of information even though I felt like it wasn't helping me back then, thanks to my autopilot nature. I had no clue of what was to come. Now I can speak of only my own case, but I am one of the millions who have dealt with this process we call grieving for our child(ren), so there must be more people than me who feel this way. Please remember that you are not alone, even though you may feel like you are, and whether you are ready to hear it or not, God is always here for you and always with you! I know I was not ready to hear it, but I am glad that it was a subliminal message within my mind, body, and soul. Even as I researched for this book, I came across comments made about the book that my daughter was a part of, *Patients at Risk*, and it made me very upset just reading the insensitive comments about the book itself. I already questioned the untimely deaths and the bluntness of untimely comments, but how dare someone comment about unbias information when there is a child involved who is not here to defend herself or tell her story? Even as I hear stories on the news about a young person passing away, all I can think of is how the family of that child feels. I immediately pray for peace and comfort for that family. I sometimes wonder, do commenters even think before they speak? Do they allow their idiocy to convey their sympathy first? Do their unsympathetic comments have to be manually pointed out? I would personally never lace up for someone else those shoes that I have walked in for years. I would never wish membership in this community of grieving parents on anyone. Despite my recollection of some of the comments, I can move forward, release such angry emotions, and proceed with the facts that God has once again revealed to me that He is here.

Commenters, He is here for you as well.

I forgive myself for momentarily becoming irate. This just shows how the grieving cycle may always show up at any given moment. We may feel anger, but it can be shortened because of the will that God has given us.

Back to the one in millions: let me advance some statistics. Evermore.org is stated to be America's voice in bereavement advocacy. Evermore.org showed that by the age of sixty, 9 percent of American parents have experienced the death of a child. The University of Texas states that by the age of fifty, 8 percent of Americans experience the same grieving process as you and me. We are now statistics. We are now part of a community, and whether we are familiar with each other or not, I would never judge you or make insensitive comments in private or public because I know firsthand what it feels like. Whatever the stats are, and however you look at grief or deal with it, whether you accept it early or not, grief is devastating. With each step of your own process, there is no wrong way or right way to grieve. I believe that culturally or ethnically, we may have a mindset of how grieving is supposed to happen or take place. Even for those of us who think we have our grief under control, some learned things are not good for us. If we are taught something but it does not fit for us, then how does that clash affect the rest of our family members, our children, and our spouses? In the long run, allowing someone to tell you how to grieve or how not grieve can hold you back and keep you from experiencing a different process along with the rest of your family members. In my case, it prevented me from connecting with my children, who are also Alexus's siblings, my husband, and with my family and the most important things to her and to myself.

ROAD TO RECOVERY

I have been on the road to recovery for quite some time now. The road I was on before recovery was called grieving the death of my child. In my case, it was the death of my newly adult child. I still feel somewhat overwhelmed at times with missing her, and in this book, I talk about the grief that I became addicted to unwittingly and that I allowed to suppress me. It took me almost eight years to change my thought process about grieving.

Once I was able to recognize and identify the pattern of mixed emotions and feelings that come with the journey of mourning, I could look it straight in the face and call it out for what it was: an addiction to grieving. The harder I tried to battle my grief alone, the harder the fight became. At times, I would give up and not fight back. I would allow grief to take over my life and my mind. After almost a decade on this path, I looked directly at all the time I wasted and said **enough is enough**. I'm here, in one piece, sharing my experience with you, hoping and praying that this information will help you in some way, shape, or form. I'm praying for your strength, comfort, and peace—mind, body, and soul.

Be patient, my dear friend, and give it all to God as quickly as you can. I also reiterate that in my experience, allow yourself to recognize that God is still around you. No matter how long it takes for you to win the battle, He will wait for you. He has already won (He has our children, and they will be okay forever) and is waiting for you to catch up to Him at the finish line. You may be thinking that I must be out of my mind. You may be asking yourself, how can I be so **over it**? How did I clear up things with God? Remember, He is for you. Also, keep in mind that what worked for me might be different for you in its details, but in essence, we all face a common situation, and we all aim

Trust in the Lord with all your heart and lean not on your own understanding.

In all your ways submit to Him, and he will make your paths straight.

Proverbs 3:5-6

to release what happened to our child and accept their death. One consistent element is the love and patience that God has for you and me.

While we may never understand the reasons behind the death of our child, Proverbs 3:5 states, "Lean not on your understanding but trust in the Lord with all your heart." Allow this message to hold an entirely new meaning for us; we are in this together. Let it begin to sink in, friend. Please do not be like me and waste years trying to understand the whys. Instead, spend that time with yourself and your loved ones in the most positive manner that you can. Know that the rest of your family is grieving as well and get through it together. There is strength in numbers, and I know about that firsthand.

Ask yourself, *What would my child want me to do, and how would they want me to live on?* How do you answer these questions?

I believe my daughter wants me to get on with my life and continue to be the best me that I can be—the me I was when she was physically present in my life. I feel this in spirit. I know I need to be the best mother and person I can be to fulfill the purpose that I was born to fulfill. I know that my daughter still lives in spirit, and she wants everyone, not only me, to live life to the fullest.

When Alexus was physically here on earth, she would ask, "What are you going to do about it?" I know now that question was preparing me for these kinds of moments, whether I like it or not, or at least I like to think that it was good preparation. Search within your mind and come up with memories and events prior to your child's passing that may hold hidden meanings or messages for you and mean more now than they did then. I believe that God places these types of concepts within us as comfort. Although the unimaginable has happened, once I got past that, all my inner trajectory makes sense in essence. God helps it make sense. Our children's purpose on earth is to make us become the strongest people in the world, and along the way, our children are placed in other people's lives to make them strong as well. But even if we are strong people, the things that happen to our children can give us weak moments, and our hearts are saddened and hardened. We are human. We are parents. We love our children deeply. We also have a purpose: to ultimately live and have our children's memories reside within us. It is said that if you remember a person, they will live on. Now that I have defeated this addiction, I am able to keep my daughter's memory alive and celebrate her life in a brighter light. Of course, I'm still saddened; that will come and go. Some days are better than others. You and I both know that. But I am in a newer, better space, and I want you to know that this time will come for you too. Look for a brighter day every time you get up, and live how your child would want you to.

Please do not get me wrong; it was not easy to get to this point, but I got here. I overcame many obstacles to get here. Thank God. Even more so, I defeated some obstacles, and guess what? I NEVER HAVE TO WORRY ABOUT the addiction of grieving because of the willpower that I have found again. As long as I place God first in my life, I know that He will help me through whatever I face if I keep the fight within me. I choose not to sit in negativity for as long as I used to. When I am faced with such challenges, I remember the strength that I found within myself. I will be okay. This strength is in you as well; it is a God-given ability, my friend, which is amazing. I believe you know this deep down inside. If you allow yourself to elaborate on the whys of your child's passing, your interpretation of the answers can consume you with guilt, anger, rage, and depression, which opens space for the enemy to get in.

BATTLE GRIEF ADDICTION

I call this battle an addiction, and I refer to the time when I allowed it to take over my life. We all grieve, but at what cost to our lives if it is doing more harm than good? For example, as I got deeper into numbing my grief by way of going on autopilot and keeping myself busy, the facts would recede. Yet as I sank deeper into the numbing process, I would find myself mad and sad—not my usual self. I would be everything I did not want to be, especially a grieving mother. I think I was addicted to the numbing part of grief. Allowing myself to be addicted to the numbing didn't work, though. As I would come back to reality, I'd cry profusely. It was a pain and still is, a heartache that would not end but is now easier to handle.

Let me also tell you that this willpower deep inside you and me is never-ending, just like the love of God—another amazing story. And I am here to testify that as much as I did not want to be bothered with God, He did not give up on me, even when I felt as if He wanted me to feel the pain and not understand why. I did not want to be His friend, but He waited on me. He never left my side, and as much as I ignored Him, He still loved me. I am explaining how I felt and what I went through in the hopes of just getting it out there, and I am astonished because He is still here, and I never thought I would feel like this—back in awe of the Lord. I'm also in awe of my willpower and of God for not losing sight of me; I reclaimed my faith!

Have you ever heard the song "Amazing Grace"? The lyrics "how sweet the sound, I once was lost, but now I'm found ..." hold a totally new meaning for me. When my daughter died, everything that I ever heard had a new meaning thereafter.

Love the Lord your God
with all of your heart and
with all your soul and with
all your mind.

I'm in awe of you, Lord.
I'm in awe of you Lord.

I will trust in You; I know
you carry me to-where
I will hurt no more.
Your greatest love I endure.

I'm in awe of You, Lord.

—Adapted from Mark 12:30

As I overpowered this addiction to grieving, including all the substances that came from it (I call them substances because I was addicted to these feelings and emotions in the same way that one is addicted to other things), I gained clarity and saw the fight I was facing. As my sight became clearer, I realized that I had grieved for so long, I had become used to it. Within the realm of addiction, a person faces many triggers, and in grieving, these triggers can be memories of your child and times spent together or thoughts about not having had enough time with them. When you allow the bad to seep into your mind and thoughts, once you get past the actual substance, you may ask yourself why you allowed yourself to get this far. Like a relapsed addict, once you get to that point you realize that even wondering is common sense, which God has given you. Be grateful for that. As the late and great Aaliyah sang, "If at first you don't succeed, dust yourself off and try again," but also try to bring a new perspective every time. Perhaps when the grief reappears, you can reassure yourself that you know how to get yourself out of the cycle, once you are able to differentiate that you can no longer stay there like before.

Throughout this book, I speak of my grieving process following Alexus's death. The tornado of grief I experienced was as follows:

DENIAL—I couldn't believe my daughter had passed away; sometimes I still cannot.

SHOCK—Shock was another form of denial but also the beginning of being NUMB, where I did not feel anything, not even the death of Alexus, not even the love for myself because of the GUILT that I had. I had not been there for my daughter when she was fading away.

Then I went back to being SAD and ANGRY at God, at myself, and at those who surrounded her death. I created theories that made sense to me at the time like OUT OF SIGHT, OUT OF MIND, trying to forget Alexus, which led me back to ANGER and

GUILT because of the methods I was using to forget my daughter. Finally, I reached a stage of SUPPRESSING all of these addictions.

This stage was followed by LOOKING AT IT, sitting back and visualizing everything that I had tried up to this point (sometimes I still sit back and look at all the things I have overcome), praying away my numbness, and transitioning to grieving and everything that it stood for with a sound mind.

ACCEPTANCE came later, but I was still on AUTOPILOT and in shock, as well as experiencing DEPRESSION and ANXIETY. The most aggressive part of the tornado of grief was MISSING my daughter and missing my other children and my marriage.

Although my other kids and husband are physically here on this side of heaven, while I was in this realm of grieving, I spent almost a decade being absent from the most important thing that God has blessed me with the chance to be the matriarch of my immediate family. These emotions were substances related to my addiction to grief. I battled with every single one and rehabilitated myself using the willpower God had placed in me because I was absolutely exhausted from not being myself—my purposed self.

Although we have lost a child in this life but not in our memories or our hearts, God has purposed us to be mothers and fathers, spouses, sisters and brothers, friends, nieces and nephews, granddaughters and grandsons, teachers, confidants, first ladies and pastors, support systems, and more importantly, prayer warriors, and so much more.

Do you know what it is like to grieve something while it is still alive? If you do not, let me draw you an unbiased picture.

When Alexus passed away, and as I went through a tornado of grief-filled emotions, I lost sight of myself and my family. All I could think about was Alexus. Not only did I put my own life on the back burner because of her death, but I also placed my entire nineteen years of motherhood, my children, and my marriage on the back burner.

I cooked up the biggest sugarcoated recipe, served it, and kept moving. I showed my own kids how to mix up this sugarcoated recipe and pass it out as well. By "sugarcoated" I mean covering up your real life as if nothing is wrong and assuming life is normal, and everything is all right. I had lost sight of all the jobs God purposed me for and turned in all those hats, wore this salesman vest, and hid my grief. As multifunctional persons, we wear many hats and hold many jobs. I sold the fact that I was sugarcoating my life and showed my children how to do the same when Alexus died. Now, perhaps the hiding was subliminal advice from family members, new or old. Maybe I had never been taught how to grieve and got lost in it while misinterpreting being blessed because we had not lost many family members to death. Maybe my God-chosen culture embraced death differently than I had imagined. So, when I shut myself out from the rest of the world, hiding my own feelings but seeming fine, I couldn't be helped anyway. At the beginning, I was so mentally and physically mad that I hated to hear people say that they were blessed because they woke up that morning. Their saying things like that offended me because my daughter did not get to wake up. I am so grateful for the prayers and the support that continued to keep me afloat. I sincerely believe that although we, you and I, lost contact with people after our children passed away, many continued to pray for us and love us from a distance. Their prayers are why we are here together, trying to keep ourselves afloat by sharing knowledge and experiences.

As I stated earlier, the different emotions and feelings I had—the tornado of grief that brought me down for a very long time—were something that I selfishly went through alone. (Remember the debris from a tornado takes time to pick up and reorganize). This was all before I even realized that my husband and children were grieving as well. This selfishness was exacerbated by the intensity of my family's not communicating as one, because we did not know how to do grieve together, much less alone. I was physically, mentally, and emotionally tired and exhausted from letting the enemy win. Was I prepared to fight for what I believed in if I had no faith left in me? Without faith and still infuriated with our creator, how in the world was I going to stand up and fight for my family and myself?

If I had suppressed my faith and if something even more tragic happened, what fight would be left in me or for my kids, husband, or other family members who needed my support? I could no longer pray at a lesser level of faith than my mother, who fought for the prayer warrior within me, instilled within me by the grace and command of God. If I suppressed my faith, would I just buckle, cave, and lose any other battle that came my way? This battle would not hold up the rest of my life, and I was definitely not going to let it defeat my motherhood, my wifedom, or my sisterhood. I am an aunt, a daughter, a cousin, and a niece. I am a person with emotional descent; I speak of my lineage, and the emotional descent is from my mother. I am a descendant of an emotional being, which has helped in my recovery from grief addiction. These emotions are what God gave me to stand up and fight with for my loved ones, for those I may never meet and whom I pray for on this side of heaven, and for myself. These emotions and feelings can get in the way of living a good life, but they can also help you be victorious, my dear friend. Use them to combat your grief. If you have no family or friends, do it for yourself. Love yourself enough to recognize that God blessed YOU with the presence of YOUR child, and that fact on its own says SO MUCH! You birthed or played a role in the life that was given to you on earth. No matter how long you had or how short-lived that was, God gave you an angel.

My daughter passed away in 2015 from pulmonary embolism. She was nineteen and very healthy at the time. Her life and death changed many people's lives, and her life and death changed my life forever. At first, it took me through a tornado of emotional events and grief, a grief I have never felt before, a grief no parent should ever have to experience. Looking back on the chain of events that happened from then until now, I was an emotional wreck and had only 50 percent of my faith. I would describe 50 percent faith as praying with half of your faith, and in saying that while praying with a false sense of hope, the absolute epitome of how not to pray.

Let me be specific. When my daughter passed away, it crushed my family and my community. But we experienced an outpouring of support that still amazes me to this day. Underneath all the support—from every support system one could imagine—my faith was suppressed. I could not understand why Alexus had been taken from ME, much less from her family and her friends. At this point, I could not even grasp my own grief, so how could I grasp anyone else's? I was undeniably and secretly upset with God, yet at the same time I was thanking others for their thoughts and prayers. Family members would ask me whether I still believed in God and how I could still go to church after what had happened. Even with 50 percent faith, I found myself getting offended and saying things like "We know better than to question the Lord." I even gave away some trinkets that held memory verses that had once been very dear to me. I was trying to hold on to the Lord as much as I could, yet I gave His words away, unfaithfully, and with less faith in my heart than I had ever felt before. And to my amazement, the recipients of my trinkets would take them and agree with me.

Many of us lose hope and faith at some point in our lives. It could be because of the loss of a job, a broken marriage, abuse, or in my case, the death of a daughter. During these losses, losing faith may seem normal because we are human. Sadly, losing faith is another easy part of dealing with loss. And even when we grasp or get ahold of our faith, there may be times when sadness sneaks back in, and of course, for parents, the worry comes back as well. In those moments, we can let the worry consume us, or we can challenge it and pray, letting go and letting God. The enemy would love for us to encounter heartache, because when we encounter heartache, we are at our most vulnerable. When we are vulnerable, the enemy seeps in and steals what little joy we may have left or creates a space to make us forget what joy we have left. The enemy can also create more negativity.

A wise man once said, "Stop running from the wilderness; run to it and just go through it!" I heard Pastor Neyland Pettis Sr. from the United Baptist Church in Oklahoma City reference Mark 9:23–24: "If you can?" said Jesus. "Everything is possible for one who believes." Immediately the boy's father exclaimed, "I do believe; help me overcome my unbelief!" I understood this sermon to talk about the faith that everyday Christians should hold. We walk around praying and smiling and holding on to complacent thoughts about ourselves, others, or even God. By definition, the word *complacent* means to show smug or uncritical satisfaction with oneself or one's achievement; to be ho-hum about something.[1] He has fully equipped us, yet we wait around trying to place blame or make excuses for tragedy or what takes place in our lives. We do not make excuses for good things, do we? So instead of running to the Lord with pure and malice-free love within our hearts, we help advance negativity and complacency. Remember that the parent in us can be sad or grieve, but let yourself grieve for a moment and resume life to the best of your ability. It isn't easy, but it is possible. As seasons change, so do the moments that we encounter. Jesus said, "Everything is possible for one who believes ..." My interpretation of these words is that death has occurred, but celebrate life and get back into the faith and stay there. Accept His comfort and peace. It is definitely easier said than done for most people, so when the man replied with "help me to overcome my unbelief," God did, and He will. He did for me.

I pushed my sorrows deeper and deeper, praying at 50 percent; remember, I was still mad at God. Yet my husband, Marlon, kept me in church. After church on Sundays, I would contribute to my grief until I forgot about what had happened to Alexus and what the pastor had talked about. After a few months of that, I tried an "out of sight, out of mind" approach. I wanted to forget my daughter so that I could deal with her passing. I couldn't look at her pictures; I didn't want to look at her pictures. As you and I both know, the death of a child is the most excruciating pain imaginable. I wanted to blunt this feeling the best way I knew how, and desperate times call for desperate measures. I was desperate.

---

[1] *A Student's Dictionary & Gazette*, 18th ed. (2010), s.v. "complacent."

Can you imagine forgetting your firstborn, or any of your children? Perhaps you did or did not. I did.

So I believed in Jesus. I prayed. I went to church. I talked to others about how good God was. Nevertheless, in the back of my mind, I struggled with my faith. I mean, how could I not when He answered so many prayers for my family, but not this one? I went through a tornado of grief, as I mentioned earlier. I was denying myself and my children the proper tools needed to pray and believe in prayer. I lost hope.

It used to break my heart to hear of any child losing their life. At times, I would be so affected that I would try to imagine one of my kids dead, but I never really grasped what a parent or family might be going through. And if I did, I didn't get past the actual timeline of grieving or the timeline that was to come for the child's loved ones. It was too hard imagining that scenario, so why even consider it to that extent? But just temporarily imagining those feelings was too much for me to understand then, so I would quickly stop them. Yet at those times, I would just stare at my kids and love them a little more that day. But then to actually go through the death of a child? The imagining didn't stop; it continued, but now I could picture each one of my children in the coffin, lying there as still as Alexus did, lifeless. Along with those images came the fear that if death was around, maybe it was still looking for its next victim. So back to anxiety it was for me. The endless grief.

Grieving added many difficult issues to my family and created much distrust among us, especially for me. How can a mother trust herself to be a good parent and do whatever she can to be the best that she can be if she does not trust others? As my children grew older and wanted to reconnect with their peers, I held a dark cloud over them and their enjoyment of life as I buried myself deeper into the emotions and feelings of my grief. I had to know my children's every move and who they were with and where they were. I hated to see my kids walk out the door for fear that I wouldn't see them again. I caused arguments when they did not answer their phones or came home late. Not able to withstand the battle, I gave up, and my autopilot tendencies increased, bringing more anger and becoming the norm for me.

I took responsibility away from my children to keep myself busy and made my children the excuse when, in fact, I was disabling them. I was setting my children up for failure and making excuses for it. I began to take over their chores and ease up on punishments and discipline, telling myself that I did not want to see my children upset or hurt. I let them get away with everything. In a sense, I was allowing them to raise themselves, yet I still could not communicate with them or help them process the pain of losing their big sister. One piece of advice I would give to any parent dealing with the death of a child is to continue to parent your other children. It is imperative to get through the cycle of grief knowing you have family grieving as well, but also maintaining the parenting that was there before your child's death.

Even though I thought I was the perfect mom and wife, I was emotionally detached and overemotional. I was angry at myself and feeling guilty. I had to release my addiction to grief because it consumed me.

My daughter deserved to be remembered, and my other children deserved more than me imagining them also being dead.

I still had four younger children who needed their mother, a husband who needed his wife, and most of all, me—I needed myself. I needed to love myself again to be able to love my family and most of all to love my God. If I couldn't take care of myself, eventually I would break down even more. I loved my family so much that I had to use them as inspiration to love myself. I had to use them as the reason that God blessed me with to have them, because without them, I think the enemy may have thought he had me totally.

My daughter Alexus had a memory verse tattooed on her neck from Philippians 4:13 which read, "I can do all things through Christ who strengthens me." I used this verse during many difficult times, and when the enemy was trying to steal my joy, I wrote a song about it.

I struggled with my faith and felt all alone, when all along He comforted my soul. He helped me and a new song I sing. I can do all things through Christ who strengthens me. I fell to my knees and felt brand new. He shifted my mind, my faith renewed. I can do all things through Christ who strengthens me

As a last resort, though I wish it had been my first resort, I forgave myself for beating up myself. I forgave all those involved in Alexus's passing and released what happened to her. I no longer could be angry at God. It just did not seem right. I knew that the longer I stayed mad at Him, the longer my prayer warrior in me would not prevail. I was tired because I had prayed for years with the apprehension of false hope or lack of faith—even when God was making miracles come to pass before my eyes. Looking back at it now, it does not even seem right. What was I asking for? Was I making a wish list and hoping my false hope was being concealed? And then if the wish wasn't granted, would I continue to blame God? No, I could no longer wish; I had to pray and fully have faith and trust in God's plan.

I am only human. God made us human, with human emotions, and I am trying to keep this recollection as honest as possible in regard to the feelings I had, good or bad, right or wrong. But at the end of the day, no matter how I was feeling or may be feeling, God is still for me, and He is still for you. I had to come clean with God. I had to make a choice. I could not teach my children how to pray with a false sense of hope. Not only would I be lying to myself, but I'd also be lying to my kids and lying to God. I would not be the liar; the devil is already good at that. He didn't need my help, but he wanted to ruin me so I could falsely lead my children and continue to disappoint myself by letting him hold me back from growth and knocking me down every chance he had. I had to be ready to answer my children's questions in all honesty, from my heart, and get back to where my faith was, in case they ever had doubts. How else would we get to heaven to see Jesus and Alexus?

While I was going through my near self-demise, I spoke to a very wise woman, my niece Meagan, who told me, "We must be as honest with God as possible. He wants us to let Him know how we feel even when it's to let Him know we are angry with Him. He already knows!" She said, "Imagine our kids hiding something from us, and we already know what they did and that they are lying to us. For what? God wants us to be completely honest with Him when we talk." She then told me to "speak to him as if He is our father because He is. We must be specific. Build that relationship with God again."

When she was talking to me about this, I was still so angry and confused that I could not hear a good thing if God himself was saying it to me; maybe He was sending it by way of my beautiful niece Meagan. He sent me many messages, and the craziest part is that when I finally prevailed and trusted 100 percent in God again, all the messages came in like a brand-new song, and He gave me this ability to remember and hear again what had been told to me over the past years. When you are angry, you cannot hear straight. How many times have we let go and let God? I'm still doing it now with my living children (and my husband and two dogs), but in all sincerity, be as upfront and honest with your creator as possible. Give the whole truth and nothing but the truth, so help us GOD!

PROCESS YOUR GRIEF

Grieving is a process full of emotion; emotion is the mental process of feelings. This can be draining in every way. Your mind is filled with memories and thoughts, which can lead to an array of cognitive recognition and some triggers. The term *cognitive* is defined as being conscious of mental activities, and *recognition* is acknowledgment of something's existence.[2] In essence, combining memories and thoughts can create anger, guilt, sadness, and so on. Now, imagine having so many thoughts and memories at the same time as feelings of grief and other emotions. Why wouldn't a normal person experience grief (a whirlwind of emotion) after the death of a child?

Burying a child does not seem normal, but it is a part of life, and we cannot be stuck in one part of life forever. We are merely humans here on earth, for a moment, a season, or many seasons. We must make the most of it because life is truly too short, as you and I both know.

As I mentioned earlier, I am in no way a psychologist nor a philosophical person. I am, however, a mother and wife who spent

---

[2] *A Student's Dictionary & Gazette*, 18th ed. (2010), s.v. "cognitive" and "recognition."

many years spiraling into the same life-stopping cycle of grief. I was tired of feeling defeated in my mind, body, and soul. Even if I felt as though the guilt and shame of my thoughts belonged to me, I would heighten my own negativity with questions like, What could I have done? What did I do to deserve this? (I would also keep hearing the judgmental people with their never-ending criticisms.) What could my daughter have done to deserve this? If you experienced petty, insensitive, and self-righteous people who surfaced after the death of your child, you know what I mean. And instead of praying for you, they catch clout by being self-righteous and keeping it moving. I am glad that I am human and that I, too, am forgiven and forgiving.

There is a thin line between gossip and truth. The devil is a liar, and he has friends who can misdirect verses out of the Bible in the most sensitive times. But back to my questions of self-hate: What could I have done to make this not happen? And better yet, What could I do to make this go away?

Now that I am eight years into the loss of my daughter, my first takeaway on grieving the death of a child is to not let anyone tell you how to grieve, but I would also reiterate and strongly suggest letting go of what happened to your child. I was afraid to let go of what happened to Alexus for fear of also letting her go. I wanted to forget her—out of sight, out of mind—but I could not let go of any of it because I was reasoning with myself with closed ears. I was still upset and lost sight of the truth: the word of God. I once was blind, but now I see another new meaning.

I tried going through this whole ordeal as if she were out of my sight because then she would be out of my mind. Lord knows I was out of my mind, too. But I quickly retracted that frame of mind because she deserved to live on in my heart and my memories. After eight long years, I grew tired of the vicious cycle that I'd allowed death to put me through. I was at my wits' end. I couldn't even mother my children or be a wife to my husband.

There will be days that lead you to cry or be angry. You might grieve regularly or unexpectedly. This is all a part of a normal process that millions of parents experience. As parents, we try to do the best that we can and lead by example. I was wrong for trying to conceal my grief for my daughter in front of my other children. I didn't want them to see me cry or be affected emotionally because I didn't want to hurt them. But in truth, I was causing more harm than good by hiding these things. It's important to allow your children to see you be as human as possible and not in a perfect light. The only perfect person is Jesus. Can you imagine walking in His shoes? Perhaps we can somewhat understand what His mother, Mary, felt like to have to bury her son. I am not even remotely trying to compare our children to Jesus, (our children are as important to Mary as Jesus is to her so in that manner I am) but I am referring to Mary's strength and how she knew what was going to happen to him.

I had a conversation with my second-oldest daughter, Aniah, who is now twenty-two. She let me know she "still does not know how to grieve, if there is even a way." Imagine a grieving child going through her most sensitive years of life not knowing how to release grief. During my conversation with Aniah, she told me that she felt as if she had been raised to be male, someone who concealed their emotions. She explained to me that the only time she really grieved her sister was when her father broke the news to her and her siblings. I was not even there, not physically or emotionally. She agreed with my assessment.

I also spoke to my middle child, Ayissa, who was eleven years old when Alexus died, and she told me she never thought she would say that she was glad it happened when she was younger because now, at the older age of nineteen, she "can't imagine how to handle it." She expressed to me that once she got older and met more peers with family members who had passed away at a young age and other family members who had lost their siblings, she questioned how she herself "would handle it at an older age." She insisted that because she was younger than those around her when it happened, she felt like she "couldn't really relate." She could only support. But what she does remember is that as she grew older, she didn't want to talk about it until she was ready.

Amannee, then eight, expressed that she wished I "would have spent more time" with her, understanding that she "grieved alone and it changed" her forever.

I also have a very strong son, Marlon II, who takes his strength from his father and from God. He is now thirteen. I am sharing my children's experiences and words here so that you are reminded, unlike me at the time of Alexus's death, that your children also need your strength. Once you emerge from your feelings or place them aside for your kids' sake—and even your spouse's sake—you can begin to build strength in numbers during the grieving process. Being with each other, talking about what happened, and keeping it real with your household about the importance of grieving as a unit and as a family is essential, because you are only as strong as your weakest link. For eight years I kept myself busy trying to keep my mind off the fact that Alexus wasn't coming back. I also took over all the chores and took a lot of responsibility away from my children. I talked myself into thinking I was doing right by letting them be kids and be comfortable. I did all the housework. And now in real time, I am struggling with myself to be patient about some things that I made them lose out on.

In the previous sections of this book, I gave many examples about myself, and I know I was wrong to think of myself as a weak person. Anyone going through so much cannot be weak; perhaps weakened, but not weak. It is time to move forward as a unit with my entire family and to openly love each other, be there for each other, and support each other because the best way to start is from within and from a place of honesty. There is strength in numbers.

The previous section also held many "self" words. Now allow me to explain some of the positive ideas using the word "I," which created my strength. I was called "strong" for so long that I believed it, and that was a good thing until I hated the word. Allow me to switch direction very briefly and note how quickly we can get distracted and how quickly we can get back to our focus if we try with one of our God-given abilities. They are there waiting for us to reveal it. Can you believe I was calling myself weak? That the pressures of being strong made me feel like I was inhuman? Was I a superhero? I absolutely was! I am a superhero, as was my mom, her mom before her, my grandmother and my aunt, my sisters, my niece, my best friend, my cousins who had lost children before me, and the countless people who have overcome grief for hundreds of years before us. If you think about it, God, Jesus, and the Holy Spirit are all superheroes, so why wouldn't we be? After all, God created us in His own image and sent Jesus down to earth in human form, making Him relatable to human feelings and emotions.

My mom, Juanita, also passed away on January 25, 2022. The death of a parent is sad on its own, full of grief. As I grieved for her, that same tornado of emotions came right back to me, along with my coping mechanisms. I realized that I did not want to be where I had been eight years ago, so I was able to control it before it started. But in doing so, I felt as if I had more control and knowledge while allowing myself to grieve properly. I also felt that when we buried my daughter, I would be able to get through anything. I would say now that burying our daughter only prepared me for more funerals. I attended a few funerals after Alexus's and was still sad yet numb. I eventually quit attending them. But each death is different; I will not deny that. I feel like it is important to deal with grief head-on and in a clear space in order to get on with the next death. The only reason I am mentioning this is to show you how once you begin using your God-given abilities, they are more easily accessible than when you are not ready. The saying "Stay ready to keep from getting ready" applies here; I know that dealing with the death of a child can be devastating, but the strength that God gives us is astonishing. Nonetheless, nothing compares to the death of a child, no matter what age the child is or how they pass away. It feels unnatural and wrong, but sadly and realistically, it is a part of the life cycle.

So now I am a superhero in human form, and my children will be as well. You are a superhero too. All you have to do is find your strength and tell your weakness to get lost, or better yet, allow God to bind your weaknesses and send them out to the abyss where He places things for us that shall not come back. Live how your child would want you to live, represent your God, and embrace yourself. Remember, crying is not a sign of weakness. I once heard that tears come from within and that once one is overwhelmed with emotion or feeling, tears empty those things out.

There is a saying "Don't bite off more than you can chew." We can all relate to that. It's normal. Do not let that get you down. Make sure you chew it up and spit it out; do anything to get rid of it. Scream if you have to. That is okay, too, and it feels good.

LOW-KEY

I took many paths of recklessness. When my daughter passed away, I wanted to lie by her side in the ground. I asked myself repeatedly, Why isn't it me in the coffin? I tried to talk myself into trading places, selfishly. I did not care about my own mental or physical health, perhaps subconsciously planning my own demise. Maybe I was LOW-KEY punishing myself and subconsciously not even thinking twice about it. I was distorted and thrown. I felt this way while still maintaining everyday duties. I was on autopilot. I walked around like I was the strongest person ever. I walked around like nothing ever bothered me when, in truth, I was suppressing every positive and negative emotion and energy I had. It seemed like the more that didn't bother me, the stronger I was. I was lost without my faith. I would listen to what people said and feel like a lot of it didn't mean anything to me or didn't apply to me. But once all these emotions began to come out at the same time, I remembered bits and pieces of how people handled similar grief, pain, fear, and worry. I'm here to say that I'm glad I heard and listened to those things. Even though my being on autopilot meant that I could not retain what I heard then, my cognition kicked in, and I am so grateful for that. Another God-given ability.

AUTOPILOT

I spoke about autopilot earlier in this book. I would describe auto-pilot as a period in my mind when I was performing daily functions and being cautious but not retaining anything. I would have conversations and interact with people but could not remember specifics. I believe autopilot to be a form of shock. For example, when a person gets hurt badly, the body does amazing things that protect them from pain. Autopilot is probably one of the best and worst mental defenses that a human has. It's good because it allows you to gain the natural strength that you need, but bad because you miss out on so much time and waste so much energy. All these processes are normal, and if we allow ourselves the proper time to heal, we can make sense of our feelings and our process. What I mean by "making sense" is that once I got through the early stages of fighting through the grief, watching my family face obstacles and not knowing how to process them, my family and I hit a brick wall as a unit, but we weren't even on the same side of the brick wall. This was all new to us, and we were still not 100 percent faithful in prayer as a family. Eventually, I was able to look back and see exactly what went through my mind, because once it started emptying itself of the chaos, things began to settle in and I finally got fed up—and you will get fed up because chaos becomes quite bothersome.

At first, as you challenge yourself to rid yourself of the chaos, it may begin to lessen, but it may try to find a crack or crevice where it can stay in your mind. Just know that that is how the enemy works. Whoever or whatever your enemy is, do not let it become you or define who you are.

As order starts to envelop your mind, it banishes the chaos more and more. Finally, when there is enough order and coordination within you, you'll find the proper weapons and tools God gives you, like in the verse at Isaiah 54:17: "No weapon formed against me shall prosper."

No weapon formed against thee shall prosper; and every toungue that shall rise against thee in judgement thou shalt condemn. This is the heritage of the servants of the LORD, and their righteousness is of me, So saith the LORD.

—Isaiah 54:17

When I first released my grief, I prayed the verse that no weapon formed against me shall prosper, and the enemy was heavy on my tail, trying so hard to get back into my mind. I became more specific and prayed that no weapon formed against my soul would prosper, that no weapon formed against my happiness would prosper, no weapon formed against my strength would prosper, and in those very moments, I regained a strength that I had lost when the devil took my joy. I wrote a song to help me combat that experience, because once the enemy is allowed to creep into the cracks and crevices of your mind—and they will try—you must be ready. My fight had just started, and I may have seemed vulnerable to the enemy, BUT there was no way I was going to literally start again. That is not what God created us to do. He created us to walk in faith and endure the many things that happen not only to us but to those around us. People we know, like you and me. Perfect strangers.

The newfound coordination sends messages throughout your mind to start emptying out the negative and whatever came with it. As grieving humans, we may perhaps have memories that have been suppressed for years, so let those come out. Be glad for the ones that God has allowed you to forget and that shall never come back, because He has bound those.

Allow me to add a detail: if you suppress something because it reminds you of something you've experienced, this process may take longer than you need it to. Challenge yourself to remember what shut down your mind, and use that as a form of self-therapy. But be cautious to not unbind what God has bound already. Before God bound the negativity that I used to cope with Alexus's passing, I could no longer go through the motions of making myself forget with self-medication and then having her death come back to me every time I would return to normal—or what I thought was normal.

I asked God to take away anything that was keeping me from mourning and grieving in the way I thought I was supposed to. I was new to this type of loss. If you recognize a trigger and have been hiding it, or rather, if you have been hiding from it, the trigger may win, and eventually you will allow it to hold you back. In this instance, when Alexus passed away, her photos and memories were triggers for me. At the time, I was so inept at being normal that I tried anything, even if it meant acting as if my child had never been born.

Stop trying to suppress anything else. It is very important to get anything and everything out of your mind that is possibly holding you back. Do not let something that is holding you back get bigger or become a trigger in any way, shape, or form. Control your triggers, and do not allow any room for them to control you. Make your mind mind you. It is possible; we are in this together. Mentally and spiritually, you are not alone. Please remember that. And just to clarify: a trigger, negatively put, is anything that makes you encounter a certain negative feeling. It can bring back feelings of remorse, anxiety, and fear, or any familiar emotion that you once carried. Triggers are known to create negative and emotional setbacks. Perhaps fill your mind with good things, and make your mind create positive triggers to quickly pivot away from the negative.

For His anger endureth
but a moment; in his favor
is life: Weeping may endure
for a night but joy cometh
in the morning.

—Psalms 30:5

LIGHT AT THE END
OF THE TUNNEL

I waited so long to see the light at the end of the tunnel. My mind was darkened by so much grief. I wasn't even having dreams. I couldn't think past the grief. Chemical-free, I was only getting three hours of sleep a night. Here, I mean chemical-ingested-free, not mentally chemical-free. Then it got to the point that I couldn't even hear myself think. I suppressed so much that my mind got quiet. I forgot what my normal thoughts were like, and I had to retrain my mind. It was not easy because the grief would try to sneak back in. But once I was refamiliarized with the strength of God and the good word that He had once instilled within me, I was able to recommit myself to winning that battle of negative feelings and emotion.

Grieving is an uphill battle but is not undefeatable. Do not let grief keep you in a repetitive cycle of doubt, fear, and worry. Arm yourself with positivity and some scriptures and some good words. God created us to worship and praise Him. "He did not create me to fear," as Anthony Brown and Group TherAPy sings. God wants us to be prepared when difficult situations arise. He is for us.

It wasn't easy for me to get back to the point I'm at now, but God doesn't give us more than we can handle, which favors and protects us. We may not like what we are going through, but once we defeat those situations, we can tell our story. I never want to go back to praying at 50 percent faith. Psalms 30:5 says that "weeping may endure for the night, but joy comes in the morning." Do not allow the devil to keep you in the night. Use your strength to get you to the morning. The great singer- songwriter Tye Tribbett explains it in his song "Only One Night Tho." It is amazing how life changes and how you feel when you have a different perspective on life after you get back to your normal state. Although life will not be the same, prayer can bring you back to a restored faith.

Sing your new song. I went through eight years of life doubting so much because of what happened to Alexus. I spent so much time on the wrong things that I forgot what right felt like. After struggling through the change, a reclaimed faith, I lived a brand-new life. I had forgotten what a good life felt like, without feeling guilty and angry. Sure, sometimes I feel angry and guilty, and the old doubt tries to climb back into my mind and heart. But when that happens, I recognize it, and I have to stand up and say who I am and who my God is and keep it moving. I introduce my mountain to my God (Pastor Neyland Pettis Sr.). Sometimes it can be tough, but most of the time it can be as easy as singing a familiar song. Sing your new song.

While dealing with the hardship of losing my faith and everything that surrounded it, I couldn't tell if I was coming or going, my mind was so polluted with the enemy. I had to literally sit down and write a song to help me combat the sneaky voices in my head. I wrote letters to my daughter and created poems and journals about what I was feeling. When God created us, He knew what He was doing. He created our minds, bodies, and souls to be so complex yet so simple. I believe that if you search within yourself, you will be amazed at how short of a time it takes to figure out how you work. Don't get me wrong—the healing process can take time. Even when you are at your heightened faith, the negative can seep in.

Devil get away from me.
In the name of the Lord
I shall believe. Devil get
away from me.

Devil shall not steal my joy.
The Lord is my rock and
He's my salvation.

Devil get thee back from
me. The way that it works
is in Jesus' name.

There may be some times
when you're feeling alone,
just call on His name
He will let you know...

(authored by Amelia)

When you hear that voice in your head telling you to get up and move around or focus on something else, listen to it. That voice, that positive voice, is another one of God's gifts.

TIME HEALS

Once Alexus's funeral was over, that chapter of my life was closed. When going through a child's death, there are steps that one goes through from the time the child passes to the time we heal from it. I call them different chapters. Not knowing how many chapters my next moments would give me, I began a new journey that I would not like but that I became accustomed to. Little did I know that it would become my new normal. My mind was so much on autopilot that I couldn't remember my daughter's funeral services. When my daughter left, I wanted to be with her and end my journey permanently. I felt like she took a piece of me with her—a piece that died with her that day. I questioned the Lord, and I wanted to give up on everything that I was raised with; I wanted to give up on church and what God stood for. When I had those thoughts, I think the enemy began to creep into my mind. How could I want to die inside and have a family that was still alive? I used to say that Alexus took 20 percent of my heart and left me with 80 percent. I became my own enemy. Looking back, I feel like I had more than just the devil as my enemy. I was chiseling myself away, slowly but surely, allowing more negativity to enter my already fragile mind. I was grateful for the support and the prayers, for family and friends and the community.

Today I am here with my family, without guilt, and it feels good. I can get on with my life. I let all of my guilt go. Once that chapter was closed, the saying "time heals" repeated itself in my mind. I had heard that saying many times prior to Alexus's passing, and when I did, I thought of it as just that—a saying. As time passes, it heals whatever a person may be going through. A heartache, a relationship change, and so on. Then I told myself that time doesn't heal; it just makes you adapt to or accept the situation. In truth, time does heal, basically in the same way that you adapt.

As I grew more into what I thought was the healing process, I changed what I thought were the rules. But the whole time, it was God giving me the knowledge I needed in a way I could comprehend. Even though my thought process was similar to that of others, I was using my own words, and I believe that is okay. Being able to identify with the sayings instead of turning them into your own words is better, once you get to that point. Identifying with the sayings is all about interpretation and the meaning of life, and the sayings that came before you were thought of long ago and will be here long after you leave. These are the sayings that you grew up with. Sometimes you cannot understand what they mean in the moment, but later you will understand the words. If you must explain something to yourself, capture the positive out of it, and use your own words. Then, when you grasp the concept, you can correlate that thought with other thoughts or sayings. It is totally human to become a self-guru. I was once told by my cousin Antonio Ochoa Jr. that "we have the authority to make our minds command our thoughts." As he explained in more depth, "God created us to have authority over our minds." When we are so devastated—weak or weakened—I believed our minds to be the enemy. Whether we are feeling doubt, worry, fear, anxiety, anger, shame, or even the combination of all grief, our minds can become so vulnerable that the negativity brought on by these emotions or feelings thicken and cloud our thoughts. Grieving is like an Oklahoma tornado. Clearly, we are familiar with the downside of the death of any loved one, but when it comes to the death of a child, no matter what age, the downside completely changes your life forever!

IS THERE AN UPSIDE?

Is there and upside? So, where there is a downside, there must be an upside, right? The upside is being at this point where you can let go and let God. The upside is being able to let go of what happened to your child and the things that led up to your child's death. I held on to all those things, thinking that if I let them go, I was letting Alexus go. When she first passed away, I was in shock and could not even grasp the concept, much less imagine that my daughter was gone. It wasn't even surreal—it was impossible. My firstborn, gone, within a matter of moments.

Another upside for me is that I am a mother of five and a wife, and I am now able to think clearly about how to mother my children and be a wife to my husband. Throughout the mismanaged time of my grievance for Alexus, I was still mentally absent in most of my mother and wife duties because I was not coherent enough, of sound mind, to fully be what I was purposed to be. I was stuck in the repetitiveness of sorting out the debris, the horrible emotions and feelings, trapped within me. Although as I sit and am of sound mind today, I still shake my head at the fact that we share these types of things. We all know the fact of the matter of even reading this book, revisiting in order to see the growth of our strength, is common and that is sad. I do still struggle from time to time and it still feels wrong to speak and think or share how I feel about my daughter's passing. I believe that only this community will really know these feelings and as we sit and have day to day conversations with others and those around us see us happy or rather we appear to be in a better space, they will not entirely understand us. I finally realized that God has been by my side for the entirety and has been waiting on me. To acknowledge, the downside was Alexus leaving earth, and the upside was me accepting her death and letting go of what happened to her. I found the upside. The upside is definitely not in her death, but rather what was to come after beating grief.

CONQUERING YOUR GRIEF

Use your pain to conquer your grief. I always said that the hardest part of death is missing the person. I believe that once you understand this part fully, you will be able to do more and hold the memories that you missed. We already know life is too short; do not make it shorter by letting grief make you miss time for things you can never get back. Another wise woman, Rachel Mendoza Pettis, told me "Do not spend time arguing or thinking of what makes you mad or upset; instead cherish the time that makes you happy." I've spent years on things I can never get back, the time lost impacting my life and the lives of my family in many negative ways. I am glad to hear from loved ones who have good messages and advice for me. I never was a good advice giver because I was always the listener in my family. I was always there to listen to the ranters and venters because I was a strong person, a strong woman. I am regaining my strength.

When Alexus left, I really didn't listen well anymore. I felt as if I'd lost much more than my daughter. We all lost her, and I was so stuck on myself, I didn't even see that. I became a recluse, stuck in my own emotions. One of the best messages God sent me came from my sister Veronica. All she said was "Breathe, Amy." As soon as I could see better—in a better light—I took all these instances and put them together and breathed throughout my battle with God's help (sister, I am still breathing). You must think of what your child would want for you. Carry your child's memories, and fight through the pain. It is easier said than done, but it is possible. I'm living proof years later and just understanding how to do this. I am not mad at God anymore. I had a talk with him and asked him to forgive me for the anger I had for Him, and I still struggled. But I am human, and the best part of being a human is that God understands that we are equipped with feelings and emotions. It is just a matter of time before we all go through them. Please let that go. I am no longer mad at the people involved in Alexus's death. I forgave them for myself. In the Lord's Prayer it says "…forgive us our trespasses as we forgive those who trespass against us…".

REALSPECT (REAL-LIFE INFO)

I spent so much time in my grieving cycle that it became normal to me. I allowed the negative to impact my mind for so long that it felt normal to me. I was suppressing the grief that overtook me for so long. I could no longer hear my inner voice that used to be like a soft white light, which had always helped me get back to reality before Alexus passed. Hearing my inner voice was another God-given ability I suppressed. But along with God, the enemy is around. As time went on, the negative became my inner voice and took control of my life. It made me think of ways to suppress this voice until my mind could no longer take it. The tricks we allow our minds to play on us are serious. Earlier, I spoke about the out-of-sight, out-of-mind method I used when I tried to forget my daughter existed. I also told myself that she was away at college, which she had been when she passed away, and that was why she was not around. I even started believing it and getting angry because she wasn't contacting me. The lies our minds tell us can seem so credible that we begin to believe them. Is that what you want your new normal to become? You know what you have been through thus far, and there are others just like you and me across the world. Allow yourself to grieve, but please do not get stuck there. It is hard to have a memorial service for your child. It becomes hard to celebrate others' milestones and accomplishments. It can and will be hard until you realize, at some point, that life must and will go on. Then it is up to you to stand up and tell the enemy who you are and who you represent. You were weakened for a moment, for a season, but let me tell you that you have a greater purpose and a greater God than any enemy ever placed on this earth—mind, body, and soul.

So, we are past the funeral, and once it is over, you hear people telling you to call if you need anything, that they'll be praying for you. Some do pray for you, because you're still here. People call and talk, but you either do not want to talk or cannot remember anything. Then the calls fall off, and you become irritated because you never answer or because people just go on with life while you are left to deal with the entire tragedy playing over and over in your mind. I was tired of grief beating me, just like an addiction I didn't want or need. I had to take a stand and beat the grief and what it stood for. I could no longer allow grief to win the battle. If you look at grief and its cycle, it makes sense for it to be a challenge, just like an addiction. If you get used to grieving and let it take over your life and your mind in more than one way, you can become too familiar with it and stuck within that cycle just as an addiction. Grieving can also follow a pattern like a roller coaster following a track. But I wanted to get off that ride. I was cheating myself and my family. And when I look back, I cannot get those times back, yet I'm here to say and to testify that it is critical to let go of what happened. Again, as I reiterate the importance of giving it all to God and keeping the good memories that He has given you, allow this repetition to spark speaking these good things into existence. In this book, I've talked about what I went through as a mother who experienced all these things. When I allowed God 100 percent back into my life, I let go and let God.

Now you're probably thinking, How could a person allow God back into their life after all this? When He first created us, He sent His only begotten son to die on the cross for us. Right? How do you allow God back in when he makes us worthy? I know God was always with me. I just had to acknowledge that part. He was waiting on me and never left my side. As I let the grief take over my life, I lost sight of that. He is here, there, and everywhere. He is for you and me. Let Him back into your life. Beat grief! A wise man once said, "I can do all things through Christ who strengthens me." Repeat it as often as you need to. I needed to repeat it, even in this book. Become familiar with the words, and when your life seems to return to the grieving cycle, take shelter with prayer and the strength that God gives you, and repeat those very words. Repeat any words that may help you stand up and fight for your sanity and for your faith. I am hoping that by the time you finish this book, your strength will be at a better place than it was when you began reading it.

BY YOUR SIDE

As I was overcoming my addiction to grief, I used many avenues as inspiration. One such avenue was listening to a variety of music, including the renowned musician Rod Wave, whose sounds are amazing and whose lyrics are justifiable and relatable. His words can be interpreted in many ways, and I was very inspired by them. He has a song called "By Your Side," and the lyrics go as follows: "…Hey there, everybody, what's it like in your city? I'm a thousand miles away, but look tonight you look so pretty … Times Square couldn't shine as bright as you … Hey there, everybody, don't you worry about the distance, I'm right here if you get lonely … close your eyes, listen to my voice, it's my disguise."

God had been by my side when I was going through it—and I mean going through it. Crying while I turned my mountain into a series of mountains. Over eight years, my life was the biggest set of mountains, yet God was still for me while I was lost because it was the enemy and myself that had led me to be lost, not found, but so lost in utter chaos that I couldn't stand myself. Imagine being blessed beyond measure and still acting and thinking in a stuck position. At that point in my life, I gave up on hope; or rather, I forgot I had given up on hope and lived life that way. Let me say that again. I was at 50 percent faith and IT DID NOT BOTHER ME!

God said, "Amy, I am going to give you the lifelines. Just grab one." He said, "I've been throwing lifelines at you for eight years, and you're still not grabbing ahold of them. And I am still here, waiting for you to recognize the ability to release your grudge with Me and catch and rekindle the flame." Faith is the light that guided me. Alexus's death extinguished my flame of faith. I allowed so much negativity to overpower my mind that the enemy could not wait for me to throw the entire torch away. Even if I had thrown the torch away, I knew someone greater was still holding it for me and waiting for me to ask for it back. God restored my soul, and He led me by the still waters. I felt every bit of those green pastures on this side of heaven. He anointed my head with holy oil. God is for us!

Please do not allow grief to overtake your faith. Please make sure to count your blessings and smell the coffee and the flowers. Live guilt-free and enjoy what you have, my friend. The smallest things can be so expensive, yet so priceless. Cherish your God-given abilities—abilities we all have. Stand up and say who you are. Quote the lyrics "My daddy is a gangster" by Rod Wave and give them a whole new meaning. They had a whole new meaning for me: Embrace your gangster! God must be the greatest and biggest gangster ever. He shows us how to fight, and when we are weary, He fights for us. The gangster in God defines the greatest movement ever in history.

I listened to "I Smile" by Kirk Franklin, a song in which he includes excerpts by Scarface, a famous rapper back in the day. He was just a gangster rapper who was trying to get his words out. That song also inspired me to smile again. I lived the longest eight years of my life being present yet absent at the same time.

As parents, our children may see or assume that our plates are full. As caregivers and everything else that parents stand for—judge, friend, provider, teacher, doctor, therapist, trendsetter, go-getter, human, robot who can break down and get fixed, an imperfect person still learning new things every day—we must tell our kids that when they need us either emotionally or mentally, we can place our plates aside and warm them back up later. As parents, we should help our children in their grieving process. We must let them know it is okay to grieve, to cry, to be upset, to sit alone, to stand together, to hug one another, and to be angry, sad, and emotional. It is okay to laugh and remember the good times and to reiterate that there is strength in numbers. My friend, grieving is all over the place. We cannot allow grief to overrun us. Get help and help each other. When you think of others going through similar experiences, once you are able to deal with your situation, start praying and reach out to them. Get through your process or pause it and help those around you. Be accepting of their process and continue your fight, or fight together, with the help of God as well. Place your superhero into your children and let them place theirs into you. Keep in mind that one day, we too will be long gone, and our children must and will carry on what we have taught and shared with them to the future generations. And if they must remix the grieving process how they need to, they will know that is okay.

There are many synonyms for addiction: habit of activity, bent, craving, dependency, enslavement, fixation, inclination, obsession, compulsion, habituation, and so on. What is your mental addiction? Mine was grieving my nineteen-year-old daughter, and for obvious reasons, I thought I was grieving alone. The better we are acquainted with the word of God, the better equipped we are for each battle or the moment of dealing. I call it "the moment of dealing" because a moment is specifically a time, and "dealing" refers to being concerned with something or coping with it. Look at your moment of dealing as a specific time frame to be concerned with or to cope with the issue in your mind. When coping with a specific issue, think of the tools that are held within your mind. Sometimes we are selfishly reluctant to give up this addiction for fear of the unknown. Or even more so, we have been addicted for so long that we've become accustomed to it—so it becomes our new normal. Is grieving your new normal? Is the complacency of this new normal okay with you? And if it is, are you complacent with your inspirations? My inspirations were sitting right in front of me the whole time, alone, yet my mind was so darkened that I couldn't see.

Thank you for allowing me to share my journey with you and together finding light that was once extinguished.

It is said that the first step to recovery is to admit you are an addict. If you feel like you could be an addict of grief, as I was, then I challenge you to take a stand and announce to yourself that you are addicted to grief and begin your steps to fight with everything you have. Take it day by day and begin to see your future for the love of your child rather than for the hate of what happened to your child. Let go of your grieving addictions. I speak of God frequently in this book to create a clearer picture than what the enemy addiction had painted for me. The enemy is still around, trying to convince me to relapse. At times, I think about it, but I remind myself how far I've come by the power of the right hand of God. I had to take a leap of faith. I believe fully that God didn't give up on me and I will not give up on myself. He didn't carry me this far just for me to turn back to the addictive ways that were creating a darkness I didn't want to be a part of. I am here, and God is here for me, and he is here for you. Give yourself some space and seek refuge in the biggest rehab facility ever known to humankind. I am a firsthand researcher, and seeking refuge worked for a person like me. Grief addiction has no prejudice against color, socioeconomic status, gender, ethnicity, or religion. It has no specificity in groups that you and I are familiar with, but it does place us in the same category.

Matthew 19:26 says, "But Jesus beheld them, with men this is impossible; but with God all things are possible."

Take your leap of faith, and do not let the enemy take any more of the faith that is suppressed within you. Set your faith free.

YOUR STORY

In the next few pages, when you are ready, write down some of the things that may help you. As this brief book is meant to be revisited, allow yourself time to remind yourself that you have the strength, wisdom, and courage to put an end to your addiction to grief. I will give an example on the first line to help you with your first courageous step.

WRITE DOWN YOUR GRIEVING SUBSTANCES, EMO-TIONS, AND FEELINGS.

One of my grieving substances was denial. I could not believe my daughter had passed away.

_____

_____

_____

_____

_____

_____

_____

_____

_____

_____

_____

_____

_____

_____

_____

_____

_____

WHAT PROCESS HELPED ALLEVIATE SUBSTANCES, EMOTIONS, AND FEELINGS?

I accepted that my daughter was deceased. I released what happened to her but kept her in my memories.

WHAT ISSUES OR TRIGGERS CAUSE YOUR HEARTACHE?

When my daughter's friends were all collecting or crossing milestones, it reminded me of my daughter missing out. I made excuses not to attend celebrations.

_____

_____

_____

_____

_____

_____

_____

_____

_____

_____

_____

_____

_____

_____

_____

_____

_____

_____

_____

_____

_____

_____

WHAT TECHNIQUES AND TOOLS CAN YOU USE TO REPLACE THE SUBSTANCES OF GRIEF THAT YOU CARRY?

I replaced my substances with courage and acceptance, and I prayed for these things so that I could celebrate things that are supposed to be cherished. I challenged myself to celebrate, and as time went on, I could appreciate happiness.

And the light shines in the darkness, and the darkness can never extinguish it.

—John 1:5

WRITE A LETTER TO GRIEF

Dear Grief,
You overstayed your time here. You have kept me stuck in repeated cycles that caused me to lose sight of my purpose of being a mother to the rest of my children and a wife to my husband. Grief, you have taken up enough of my time, and it is time for us to part ways. Grief, you are a part of life, but so am I. I must get on with my life.

Dear Grief,
You almost visited me today, but I had things to finish. You are real, and I am noticing you frequent families no matter what age. I had a somewhat good day, and you almost had nothing to do with it. As I write my own feelings and seem to have a normal letter-writing session with you, I just want you to know that you have made me who I am today and that I am stronger than before. I do not call you my friend, but we have been through some things together. It is because of you that I can revisit my strengths and stay in control.

Sincerely,
A Stronger Mother

_____

_____

_____

_____

_____

_____

_____

_____

_____

_____

_____

_____

_____

_____

_____

_____

_____

_____

_____

_____

_____

_____

_____

_____

_____

_____

_____

_____

_____

_____

_____

_____

_____

_____

_____

_____

_____

_____

_____

_____

_____

_____

_____

_____

_____

_____

_____

I am praying for you. I hope this book helps you and you are able to fill the pages with your own thoughts and feelings. I hope you can then go back and, if necessary, read through what you've written and see how far you have come and be amazed with yourself. I still find myself reading back through this book because doing so does help me get through some of my grieving issues. Although we would never wish these experiences on anyone, they are our harsh reality: we are part of a community of parents who have experienced the death of a child. Perhaps one day you will find yourself inspiring the next parent. When I started my journey, I would never have seen myself at this point, and I love my daughter and everything she still stands for. I love myself as well. I know one day she will be glad to see me and I her, and we will talk about the courage I found to continue my life and carry her memories.

My AK, until we meet again.

In writing about grief, I hope my story can help parents and loved ones who are struggling with the death of a child. No matter the child's age, their death seems unnatural. Untimely. It hurts, but you are not alone; the world is full of people like us. I am here to share my story with you and explain why I had to break my addiction to grief for my child, Alexus.

After going through the whole ordeal, I told myself that I needed to finalize this process that we all call "grief." I had to be the mother that my other kids needed. I needed to be the strong and courageous woman that God put me on this earth to be—the woman I was before Alexus died.

I wrote this book with the hope of helping others understand their own grief and find their way through the concepts that grief has imposed upon us all. In doing so, it helped me with my own grieving process in more ways than I could have imagined.

AUTHOR BIO

Amelia Ochoa-Dockins was born in west Texas but raised in the greater Oklahoma City area. She is a mother of five and is married to a United States Army veteran. Throughout Amelia's life, she has been faced with many obstacles and has hurdled them all with and by the grace of God. Her primary interest is motivating others. She firmly believes in self-motivation and sharing inspiration to maintain a realness and assure others that they are not alone in their dealings. "Life stories and lessons make us relatable, a unity for strangers within a community," says Amelia.

Amelia is a poet and songwriter and is currently working on gospel songs and a series of children's books created to mend the mental. Another perspective that resides within Amelia is to challenge the self to seek the brighter side of everything and trust in God. Her motto is *"Keep your head up and your faith higher."*

Amelia and her family have also founded the nonprofit Team AlleyKat AK12 Foundation in memory of Alexus Ochoa-Dockins. This nonprofit transfers the legacy of Alexus while creating diversity. It promotes the same work ethic instilled in Alexus at a young age, her love for life, and her love for others, along with the inspiration that is always felt by her spirit. The family uses basketball as a form of unity, as well as mentorship and counseling to help youth recognize and maintain the necessary tools they hold within themselves to conquer any challenges that life may bring them.

www.ingramcontent.com/pod-product-compliance
Lightning Source LLC
Chambersburg PA
CBHW050505290526
45786CB00006B/2443